AMERICA CHALLENGED

THE WALTER E. EDGE
LECTURES, 1960

AMERICA CHALLENGED

By William O. Douglas

ASSOCIATE JUSTICE,
SUPREME COURT OF THE UNITED STATES

1960

PRINCETON UNIVERSITY PRESS
PRINCETON, NEW JERSEY

133 000

TO ROBERT MAYNARD HUTCHINS
WHO HAS HELPED US
KEEP ALIVE THE SPIRIT OF FREE INQUIRY
IN TROUBLED DAYS

FOREWORD

AMERICA CHALLENGED is the second of the Walter E. Edge Lectures in Public and International Affairs, the first to be published in book form. Though small in size, the volume is large in substance and urgency. It fittingly introduces to the wider audience outside the University this now annual lecture series which was established by the Edge family in 1957 in honor of the late Walter E. Edge.

Governor Edge held many positions of public importance during his lifetime, including being United States Ambassador to France, United States Senator, and twice chief executive of the State of New Jersey. Inclination and opportunity made him a Republican in his politics, while Justice Douglas found his party allegiance and preferment among the Democrats. Yet this conjunction too is fitting. For in these lectures Justice Douglas's concern reaches, as did so often Governor Edge's, both far beyond political partisanship. The issues he treats, the needs he sees, the aspirations he expresses are not the monopoly of either national party today. They are, or should be, the concern of all thoughtful men. The substance of this book, then, is political only in an older, deeper sense of the word than is now common. Its focus is upon matters which relate intimately to—and threaten fundamentally—the moral, intellectual, and spiritual tap-roots of the national community which is our *polis.*

It would be presumptuous in this Foreword to attempt to introduce Justice Douglas, who is so well known both to Americans and to people the world over. It is characteristic that the dominant theme of *America Challenged* is dissent: dissent from complacency, mediocrity, illusion, the tendency to drift without purpose, wherever they occur. A passionate devotion to freedom, to the dignity of the human person, to equality before the law here bespeak that eternal, thoughtful vigilance which is, as the Irish jurist Curran said two hundred years ago, the condition upon which God has given liberty to man.

The universities of the western world have had, and must have, an important role in furthering these great causes. In these lectures Justice Douglas presents challenges to America and Americans generally, but many of these challenges bear specifically on universities.

In his first lecture he is concerned primarily with the debilitating effects of conformity. In recent years this virus, this acceptance of the easy and the commonplace, has been especially noted seeping into the attitudes of our young people, to limit their aspirations and make their responses be at minimum risk; though youth is, after all, a proper time for revolt, for assertion, for high aspiration. Competition itself may in certain conditions, as Justice Douglas points out, tend to breed mediocrity, and the intense competition our young men and women today face—in gaining admission to college, in college, and afterwards—may make them afraid to chance being different. Surely universities must combat this tendency. They must make room for, and even welcome, the student or scholar with unusual or startling ideas. They must make the educational experience as kinetic of the processes of mind and of self-won judgment as possible: which means as far as possible removed from, raised beyond, that merely passive absorption and regurgitation of knowledge which produces "good grades" and little more. They must provide for free expression of all kinds of new and unconventional thoughts and see, too, that these face the test of free and rigorous criticism. They must at the same time preserve the spirit of urgency and able striving which today inspires many of our students to far more advanced work than those of an earlier day.

The private universities, being less subject to shifting drifts of public opinion and political pressure, should be especially able to provide oases where individuals can grow, in mind and spirit, in resistance to conformity. This was clearly shown by the outspoken resistance of at least some of these universities to the aberration of McCarthyism, which Justice Douglas discusses. It is shown also in the degree to which they (at least some of them) continue to seek to challenge the student to individual achievement of a high order, leading him to extend the range of his vision and come to know the searching powers of mind.

In his second lecture Justice Douglas considers the place of the United States among nations and again presents challenges of specific importance to universities. He brings out forcefully the need to know more—and more deeply—about the underdeveloped areas of the world, especially through their languages, in order to help them raise their standards of living and nourish such ideals as we hold of freedom for the individual and of equality before the law. I am glad that Princeton University has done and is doing much in this field—for many years through its Near East Program, and more recently in its growing program of Asian studies. Princeton University Press has published no small number of notable works on these subjects, stemming from our own faculty and elsewhere. But here and in all our universities there is much yet to be done, as Justice Douglas clearly shows.

I have naturally chosen to touch on a few—and only a few—of those aspects of these lectures that apply specifically to universities. But Justice Douglas's words are clearly intended for Americans generally. The main challenge presented to all of us, his countrymen, is to see ourselves and the rest of the world as clearly as we can; to understand the main directions of significant events; and then to dare to act with foresight and with purpose. The understanding he asks of us centers particularly on a live sense of the importance of freedom of the individual. The challenge thus is to our conscience, to the moral and political (in the deeper sense) conscience of the American people, as well as to our minds. In the circumstances Justice Douglas depicts, it must be our hope that American universities can help provide both the framework of ideas in which effective action can be taken and the skilled, thoughtful, resolute men who will carry out the needed sorts of national and international programs to their fullest extent.

ROBERT F. GOHEEN
President's Room
Princeton University

CONTENTS

AT THE CROSSROADS

W E AMERICANS are at a fateful crossroads of history. We are smug and complacent as we enjoy the highest standard of living in the world. Yet we drift dangerously; and if present trends continue, we will be a second-rate power in the world.

We are dropping far behind in meeting the social and educational needs of the country. Our school system is inadequate. Our teachers are underpaid. Research on disease lags. Slum clearance and urban development suffer. Though our population is burgeoning, our recreational facilities are inadequate and little is being done about them. We are reducing year by year our wilderness areas and making cesspools out of our rivers. We are far behind the Russians in exploring space. Their rate of growth is much greater than ours. We have indeed no national growth policy. Yet unless we launch one we will never be able to handle continuously the great expenditures for military purposes and the increasing amounts needed for social and educational ends.

When it comes to world problems, we are losing the contest. The missile lag is obvious. Less obvious is the fact that while the communists are organized and prepared to evangelize the world, we are not. The Russians can send over 10,000 agricultural experts and as many doctors abroad tomorrow. How many can we send? The answer will be critical because Asia and Africa are changing. Young, new nations are emerging. They will walk on weak legs and will need help and guidance. Will they have our experts to lean upon or will they turn to the Russians?

We live in the big white house on the hill that is quite distant in thoughts and actions from the slums below us and around us. The bulk of the people of the world live and work for revolution and change. We who have arrived and who enjoy our leisure and security are not in tune with these new voices; we and they speak different languages.

The tragedy is that while the world needs leadership in revolutions, we have come to regard the word with suspicion. We—who have the most glorious revolutionary history of any nation—have let the standard be carried by the communists.

For some years we have been lulled by resounding slogans and reassured by those in high places that all is well. Yet civilization has never been in greater danger. The illusion of security still seems to obsess us though we walk the edge of the abyss.

We have the character and intelligence to repair the damage and prevent our country from becoming a second-rate power. But to do so we must understand what has happened in the world; and we must act at once.

THE INDIVIDUAL AND
THE CROWD

THIS default of ours begins at home. It involves not one but many influences. They have been long in making. They have robbed us of imaginative plans and bold action. We move more and more with the crowd and are infected with its mediocrity. The mediocrity of the crowd threatens indeed to condition our management of internal problems and our approach to the world situation.

In the last thirty years we have seen entire societies forced into a single mold dedicated to one ideal, and moving to the impulse of one thought. The communist regimes have brought control of the crowd to a high point of perfection. They have used censorship, tight control of the media of mass communication, repetition of falsehoods. They have developed highly doctrinaire and orthodox citizens.

It is my fear that we have drifted or been propelled to similar fixed patterns of thought. In fighting communism we have developed totalitarian attitudes and compulsions of our own. Moreover, the collective patterns of economic life have been on the increase. Collective action may in large degree be necessary so that advances in science and technology may reach the masses. The Indians have a word for the person whose activities and thinking depend on another. He is *para-*

tantra. In opposition is *swatantra,* which means one who has control and power of action over himself. In Indian terms the struggle of this century is between the two forces—for submission, subservience, and conformity on one hand, and for independence, individuality, and dissent on the other. It is indeed a world-wide phenomenon. And too often what takes place here mirrors what happens elsewhere. We tend to mimic the tactics and attitudes of our adversaries. It seems at times as if we were almost hypnotized by the movement of the snake's head.

This development makes all the more important the need to preserve in this highly organized society, individual freedom and initiative—and the right to dissent.

Dissent

The first reported decision[1] of the Supreme Court was rendered by a divided Court. Georgia had asked for an injunction against distribution of funds in a lower federal court, claiming a right to them. While the Court granted the injunction, Justices Johnson and Cushing dissented. And that tradition of the dissent is a vital one to this day.

The right to dissent is the only thing that makes life tolerable for a judge of an appellate court. It is essential to the operations of a free press. The affairs of government could not be conducted by democratic

[1] *Georgia v. Braislford,* 2 Dallas 402.

standards without it. It is a healthy influence in every classroom, on every board of education, at every council meeting. It is the right of dissent, not the right or duty to conform, which gives dignity, worth, and individuality to man. As Carl Sandburg recently said, "There always ought to be beatniks in a culture, hollering about the respectables."

The right of revolution is, of course, deep in our traditions. Though we have mostly forgotten it, one State, New Hampshire, has it embedded in her Constitution. Article 10 of New Hampshire's charter not only emphasizes the right to affirmative action but goes on to denounce submission to tyranny. "The doctrine of nonresistance against arbitrary power, and oppression, is absurd, slavish, and destructive of the good and happiness of mankind."

We have drifted away from that attitude. During the last two decades mass opinion has been shaped to fit narrowing molds; orthodoxy and conformity have had less and less respect for our ancient liberties; the climate has been less favorable to revolt.

Anxiety and Insecurity

The age is one of anxiety and insecurity. The forces against us are not imaginary ones. An armed communist state, warheads of atomic bombs, missiles that come faster than radar can detect—these are grim realities. A nation usually loses its liberties under the pressures of fear or under the anxieties of actual war. Every ruler or leader, every prosecutor or judge, every legislator who has denied the citizen freedom has been propelled by the feeling of great urgency. Emergencies mount and become an excitable fact in the public mind. Everyone sees the crisis through his own spectacles and doubtless deems his motives the most patriotic of all. Certainly the Federalists who sponsored the Alien and Sedition Acts in 1798 thought they were acting in the nation's best interests. They feared that subversive newspapers would "paralyze the public arm and weaken the efforts of Government for the defense of the country." William Cobbett proclaimed, "Do not the Jacobin fiends of France use falsehood and all the arms of hell and do they not run like half famished wolves to accomplish the destruction of this country?" There was the First Amendment guarding freedom of speech and of press which Jefferson and other Republicans said made the Alien and Sedition Acts unconstitutional. But there were clever constitutional lawyers then—as now—who found a way around the First Amendment. They proclaimed that self-preservation was also a power of government and that it necessarily qualified every other power. The Constitution, said Timothy Pickering, Secretary of State, was established "for the protection and security of American citizens, and not of intriguing foreigners." And a distinguished judge of that day spoke up to say, "Those who corrupt our opinion are the most dangerous of all enemies."

The Alien and Sedition Acts were not long lived. But the chapter they wrote has been repeated several times in our history. We have relived it in a vivid way in the past decade.

Loyalty Programs

Benjamin Franklin early observed that loyalty oaths were "the last resort of liars." Abraham Lincoln later said, "On principle, I dislike an oath which requires a man to swear he has not done wrong. It rejects the Christian principle of forgiveness on terms of repentance. I think it enough if a man does no wrong hereafter." Experience with loyalty oaths both in England and later on these shores should have taught us that enforced loyalty oaths are very poor guides to future good conduct. Yet since World War II many kinds of loyalty oaths were adopted for federal and state positions. Hundreds of local units of government used them. Oaths were exacted from voters, occupants of public housing projects, teachers, recipients of public welfare, union officials, those seeking tax exemptions (such as religious groups[2]), and even from boxers and wrestlers.[3] Beyond the oaths were the numerous committees, commissions, and boards active in loyalty testing. These

[2] See *First Unitarian Church v. Los Angeles*, 357 U.S. 545.
[3] Hyman, *To Try Men's Souls*, 1959, p. 338.

inquiries went beyond past and present conduct that had relation to subversion and embraced a wide range of activities (including psychiatric treatment) which were thought to make one a poor "security risk." The figure emerging as the ideal public servant was a faultless, correct, proper, orthodox—and I might add—dull character. The comparison of the ideal with the automaton became pitiless as the loyalty testing moved from the realm of conduct into the zone of ideas and beliefs.

One measure of our intolerance was the wide scope given to questions under the loyalty program for government employees. We are raised in the Jeffersonian tradition that what a man thinks is not the government's business; it is only his actions that he is accountable for. And we were brought up to think that he is not accountable to government for any actions that do not violate some law of the land. Consider then the following questions in a loyalty investigation of a government employee during recent years.

Q. "What were your feelings at that time concerning racial equality?"

Q. "Do I interpret your statement clearly that Negroes and Jews are denied some of our constitutional rights at present?"

Q. "The file indicates that you were quite hepped-up over the one-world idea at one time. Is that right?"

Q. "At one time or two you were a strong advocate of the United Nations. Are you still?"

Is it possible that in America one's belief in equality of all people or in the desirability of the United Nations can be equated to disloyalty or subversion—or even be relevant to those issues?

Further examination of this employee called for his opinion on Franklin Roosevelt, Norman Thomas, and Henry Wallace.

Another employee was suspect in a loyalty hearing when charged with having studied the Russian language with a Russian friend.

Q. "Did you ever take any lessons from anyone on the Russian language?"

A. "No, sir, no formal instruction."

Q. "You'd categorically deny that if somebody would say that you did?"

A. "Absolutely. Undoubtedly he'd tell us a common word—I know that 'da' means—it means, 'yes.'"

Q. "But you never attempted to take lessons in the Russian language?"

A. "No."

Q. "Who gave lessons to your wife?"

A. "She got these records. There was a Berlitz record of somebody's and she took the address from that. There was a neighbor of ours, two doors down, who gave her a lesson in it and she went to the Unitarian

Church, I believe, for lessons also. She'd take a couple of lessons and quit and start in with somebody else."

His views on government ownership were also deemed relevant to his loyalty. Yet we know that some of the most articulate proponents of democratic values at home and abroad have been socialists.

One employee ran the gauntlet on "liberalism."

Q. "What does the word *liberal* mean in your estimation? Doesn't it mean connected with communism and Russia?"

This line of questions was typical of the reign of intolerance which possessed us after World War II. Men and women were indiscriminately smeared; trial by investigation became a pattern of conduct; *innocent* association with subversives, plainly protected by constitutional guarantees,[4] was not differentiated from *knowing* association. Sinister meanings were imputed to a person's exercise of his constitutional right under the Fifth Amendment, even against the warning that "The privilege against self-incrimination would be reduced to a hollow mockery if its exercise could be taken as equivalent either to a confession of guilt or a conclusive presumption of perjury."[5] Blacklists flourished not for what people had done but for what they had believed or thought.

There were some protests to these invasions of pri-

[4] *Wieman v. Updegraff*, 344 U.S. 183, 190f.
[5] *Slochower v. Board of Education*, 350 U.S. 551, 557.

vacy. But we as a people did not revolt. Some did not speak up for fear they would be tarred by the same brush. The desire to get votes, by beating the drums and producing hysteria, recruited many to this regime of intolerance. One could probably count on the fingers of his two hands the newspapers that held the line, exposed the un-Americanism of these procedures, and denounced those who placed "a badge of infamy" on people by means of press releases or pronouncements in committee hearings. The truth is that we became insensitive to this type of injustice.

We have paid a heavy price for this invasion of the realm of conscience and belief. Those tagged with disloyalty or those slurred by the charges of it were virtual outcasts. Holders of the Ph.D. degree ended up working on railroad section gangs. Men and women who had spent years preparing for some branch of the public service had to put their careers behind them and seek employment in business or establish businesses of their own. But the arms of the loyalty boards were long. The business enterprise that worked on government contracts was also subject to scrutiny; and its employees came under the watchful eyes of F.B.I. investigators and loyalty boards. The casualties ran into the thousands. Only an infinitesimal number of employees was truly subversive. The victims in the main were nonconformists who once had been indiscreet or who had been so bold as to have unorthodox or un-

popular beliefs at some points in their lives, or asso-
ciates or friends who were "leftist." Few had either
the resources or the stamina to fight the charges. Most
of them resigned and became anonymous victims of
the reign of intolerance.

The damage done was not restricted to them. Their
fate was telegraphed to every sensitive mind. A generation of youngsters became aware that there were great
risks in being unorthodox and in failing to conform to
the patterns of standardized thought that were slowly
taking shape. A youngster on the way to the top might
lose his place on the escalator if he were too much of an
individualist. He might lose out even in such competitive projects as a Fulbright scholarship! The conse-
quences were far-reaching; and we have not recovered
from them. One effect was to make our foreign service
unattractive to many imaginative young men and
women. Another was to stifle reporting by those abroad.
Most youngsters at our numerous listening points were
reluctant to depart from orthodox lines, to challenge
traditional thinking, to put the communist threat in
new perspective. We suffered greatly in intelligence and
in insight. Another effect was a rapid decline in registra-
tion for Russian language courses. At a time when we
should have been studying the Russian language *en
masse* in an effort to know and understand this new
and powerful competitor, we were driven away by fear.

Relations to the Communist World

Our relations toward the communist world suffered greatly. Lines of communication were cut; we did not mingle in their circles; they were the devils we were to avoid. Yet they were and are a vital part of the world and the problem of finding ways to survive with them is the greatest one facing our civilization. Mingling with them—getting to know them—arguing and debating with them—these things should preoccupy us. Yet it was not always safe even to welcome a visitor from communist lands, though he came bearing high professional credentials. In the Spring of 1959 I was at the Law School of the University of Wyoming. I had been preceded by a lawyer from Poland. He had no sooner reached the campus when the committee in charge got a call from the F.B.I. wanting to know who was responsible for extending the invitation. The whole American tradition concerning academic freedom rebels at the very thought of the police invading the sacred precincts of the classrooms or lecture halls.[6]

This Mechanized Age

Those who go to the bazaars of the East will find the last remnants of a great artisan class. They are creative; each is very much an individual; there is no

[6] See *Adler v. Board of Education*, 342 U.S. 485, 510; *Sweezy v. New Hampshire*, 354 U.S. 234, 250, 262.

standard of uniformity to which they must conform. In the West, however, machines have to a degree moved men closer to the role of automatons. They move and act in unison; their tasks are more and more mechanical; the individual is transformed into a statistic. This mechanized society of ours throws its weight against the development of a society that honors the individual. The new regimes of science under which the western world lives encourage, indeed require, teams working in unison. Even a scientist is a small fraction of a pool of scientists working on a problem, and his creation or contribution is often lost in the joint endeavor. Less and less does man stand on his own; he works as a unit of a vast laboratory team or of an unseen bureaucracy in business or industry. The more organized a society, the more time workers, whether manual or managerial, spend on routine. Captives of routine are usually not the material out of which sparkling individuals are made.

Our Bureaucracies

Another reason for the decline of dissent is the growing tendency for American democracy to become polarized in four large bureaucracies: (1) the vast civil regimes that possess our government; (2) the mighty military cabal whose reach into our affairs becomes greater with each national budget; (3) the bureaucracy of the management that controls our five hundred leading corporations; (4) the bureaucracy of the unions whose domains have reached large proportions. There are clashes and contests within and between those rival groups; but each tends to breed conformists, not dissenters. The members of these groups are talented, and many of them are idealistic. Some of them were at the beginning of their careers creative innovators. Some within the boundaries of their own specialties think in revolutionary terms, as did those who unlocked the secrets of the atom. Yet these regimes produce a conservatism that stills dissent on the larger public issues. Men entering the ranks of this bureaucracy become extremely discreet when it comes to new ideas in law, economics, and politics. They become champions of the course of action that draws the least criticism. They are not the ones to pick up the cudgels on Little Rock or lead the debate on recognition of Red China. Advancement in the managerial ranks of these bureaucracies calls for discreet and disciplined men who do not become embroiled in controversial issues that sharply divide our society.

It is easy for a youngster to get and keep a good job in these large bureaucracies if he accepts political and social conformity. And so he tends to expend his major intellectual effort in becoming adjusted to submission, not to dissent. The preeminence of these four groups in our lives helps produce men that go with the crowd.

Emphasis on Materialism

Our stress on mass production and rising standards of living has emphasized man as an economic entity who must be fed and housed and clothed. Francis J. Grund, writing in 1839 in *Aristocracy in America*, complimented our people on the vastness of our material interests. "It is certainly a matter of rejoicing," he said, "that there should exist at least one country in the world emphatically to be termed 'the land of beef and pudding, clean shirts, and whole stockings for all.'" But he added, "In these things does not yet consist the ultimate happiness of a people or its capacity for great and generous action." The trend, however, during the century since he wrote, has been more and more to material standards. And Madison Avenue experts have dinned into everyone's ears the bright and happy future that will exist if each of us will only drink, eat, sleep, ride, exercise, and think in the prescribed way. It is a uniform society that Madison Avenue promotes, a society engaged in rather primitive conduct, with little or no spiritual or intellectual glow to it. The great financial rewards go to those who can train people in understanding and manipulating response and behavior patterns. So we have put our brains to work searching for means to manipulate man to this end or to that.

This is a new form of totalitarianism, and almost as

debilitating as any other. It has made us mass-minded. It has, moreover, taken much of the purpose out of individual lives. We eat well; we change suits often; we view the television shows which Madison Avenue has produced; we see as the hero the man who is proper and correct in all respects and who thinks the right thoughts. But what purpose is left in this soft, easy life where man is pampered and protected and groomed to be just like all other men?

Mencius said, "Heaven, when about to charge a man with a great trust, will try his soul with bitterness, subject his bones and sinews to toil and his body to hunger, reduce him to nakedness and want, and bring his enterprises to naught. Thus his mind is made active, his character tempered, and his weaknesses are made good." What Mencius discerned some three hundred years before Christ is probably the life story of many people of genius since his day. Toil, anxiety, sacrifice, conflict—these shape lives that are meaningful and creative.

Education

Much of our education avoids troublesome facts and trains students for a world that is conceived as having no deep conflicts. The so-called "progressive" school leaves the individual to find his adjustment to society and advocates personal experience as the teacher. Education becomes merely the opportunity to have pleasurable experiences. The great disciplines of the classics, of mathematics, of history, are de-emphasized and the individual seeks the level where no challenging problems exist. This again is a step towards the self-adjusted automaton who may find a niche in some regimented society but who is never brought to the peaks of idealism and heroism and who never knows the reaches of evil and good or the ingredients of tragedy, sacrifice, or fruition. Only where the disciplines are severe and the whole spectrum open to study do we develop people who have a deep personal feeling about the direction of their lives. Those who have strong convictions, those who have awareness and refined sensibility, are the products of exposure to the many facets of life.

Even in our colleges we have tended to reach the lowest common denominator of acceptable viewpoints on social and political issues. In law, economics, political science, and history we have often withdrawn to noncontroversial positions where a narrow segment of life can be taught without danger of criticism. This shuns ferment and turmoil; it produces serenity of mind; none can accuse us of trafficking in ideas that are dangerous. But it gives us mediocrity. Subjects that should be explosively controversial are dispensed as tranquilizers.

A college president viewing the sad condition of many educational institutions recently said in a facetious vein, "The job of a president is now three-fold:

finding parking space for the faculty, football for the graduates, and sex for the students."

Television

And note what television has done. This brilliant scientific achievement has been debased by catering to the lowest common denominator among us. The advertisers in effect control it and they desire that their wares not be associated with any controversial issues. And so they seek the level of broadest appeal and end up with supine and depressing programs. Think of the potentialities of television if it were visualized as a national university of the air. Then the great literature of the world could be brought to us in vivid terms. Music and art, poetry and literature, history and economics could be added to current news and sports events to make television a powerful educational force in the nation. It could help us become adult and mature. Instead its pressure in every living room is on the side of infantilism and mediocrity. The recent frauds disclosed in some of its programs were of course insults to everyone. Equally insulting is the manner in which television caters to moronic standards. Captive of Madison Avenue, television makes millions out of our capacity to endure mediocrity. Its influence is on the side of orthodoxy and conformity. It does not cultivate a society given to debate, soul-searching, or dissent.

Television has also reflected the decline in respect of

our Bill of Rights. The police are extolled; the rights of man downgraded. This is a symptom of a larger malady. One bit of evidence, not commonly noted, is the fact that the annual budget of the F.B.I. is over twice as large as the annual budget for the entire federal court system.

Dominance of the Military

World War II pitched military men into a central position of control over our lives. And their prestige allowed them to push more and more into critical positions when peace arrived. Their domination mounted as increasing billions were allotted to defense. The spending of forty-five billion dollars a year is a force of tremendous power. A part of its impact is the way it has shaped our thinking, directly and indirectly. We have become more and more military-minded as our economy has become more and more geared to military projects. There has been a conspicuous trend to move the military into policy positions. This danger-ous and dramatic break with American tradition has been largely accepted. Only a few muted voices have been raised in protest. Books such as *Soldiers and Scholars* (1957) by Masland and Radway even go so far as to show how the military can be better educated to fill these policy roles.

Yet our military-mindedness is the most crippling in-fluence in our world relationships. Much of the evil which came out of World War II stemmed from the paramount influence of the armed forces in setting war objectives. It is epitomized today by the fact that each of the armed forces has its own State Department within its organization. Bismarck's greatness was in his ability to hold the Prussian generals in check, to subordinate a military machine to foreign policy objectives. Even war is political. The American military mind seems not to understand that the enemy of today can be the ally of tomorrow. And we as a people fall into the goose step stirred by dreams of military solutions of these intensely political questions.

Foreign Affairs

Deep and permanent changes and cleavages are taking place in Africa, the Middle East, and Asia. Yet those changes have not been greatly reflected in our own educational programs. We are so deeply imbedded in our own culture that we have failed to realize—and adapt our educational programs accordingly—that there is no meaningful American culture today which omits Africa, the Middle East, and Asia. Professor John K. Fairbank of Harvard recently dramatized this thought by saying: "We actually need more screwballs and misfits, more people, for example, who look American but think Chinese." The same can be said about the Turkish, Persian, Russian and Japanese cultures. Foreign languages, such as Chinese and Russian must be introduced at an early age—say ten—in our schools, so that the oncoming generation can learn to think in dimensions now largely unknown to us. A central challenge of the age is for Americans to become the great linguists of the world. There are, however, several dozen languages of the world that we are not yet qualified to teach.

This suggestion of starting foreign languages at an early age is not new. The Soviets are doing it, beginning with eight-year-old students in certain of their schools. Hindi, Urdu, Arabic, Chinese, Persian, Turki are some of the languages taught both in Soviet primary and secondary schools; and at the university level extensive educational projects have been established for teaching history, culture, geography, and economics of the country or area along with the language. There are Russians who now can address any people in the local language. How many of us could give lectures in Russian at Moscow, in Urdu at Lahore, in Bengali at Calcutta? The numbers are so few that the condition is shocking. Yet that is one reliable measure of our neglect of the world problem.

In foreign affairs we have developed a keen sense of negativism. We are opposed to this and that; we are wholly anti-communist. We do not see the world problems in affirmative terms. We want to suppress trouble with bombs or to buy time with large grants of money.

We have no vision of the new world that is in revolution and sorely needs leaders. We have let the communists take the leadership by default. The communists retain the initiative. All we do is to react to their moves. Many among us get a feeling of security merely by marshaling arms and men and chanting worn out slogans that do not fit this day and age. Yet these things are woefully inadequate for today's crisis.

Americans probably got emotionally fatigued from the rapid series of emergencies in the 30's and the world war in the 40's. Sustained effort over long years is difficult. There comes a time when people want to push worries aside and have fun. The tragedy is that this point in the cycle was reached in the late 40's when our military took over vast powers. The preeminence of the Armed Forces (each with its own State Department, I repeat) is another reason for the mounting trend to uniformity that has plagued us.

Whatever may be all the causes, dissent has been on the decline. The pressures for conformity have been enormous. The happenstance that one's conviction momentarily coincides with the party line of the communist group is enough to still many voices. The risks in private affairs are too great for youngsters, seeking advancement or professional preferment, if one gets into step with the wrong group.

There is some reaction against goose stepping in every country that experiences it. Soviet Russia and

China take the lead in requiring submission of the masses to the gospel of the party. Yet there is some revolt against it in those lands. There is some vocal dissent even in China. Ma Yin-chu, President of Peking University, recently spoke out against the anti-birth control policies of his Communist government. He argued for decrease in the rate of population growth and for increase in the productivity of the labor force. Otherwise, he stated, the people will eventually be filled with "despair and discontent"; and "though the result may not be the same as what happened in Poland and Hungary, it will inevitably bring many headaches for the government." Thus does a teacher, trained at Yale and Columbia, raise his voice against regimentation. The so-called "freedom writers" in Russia have been chafing under the discipline of the party. A few, notably Pasternak, broke through the barrier. Most don the caps of conformity. But as the author Paustovsky recently said, it is depressing when authors have an "unwillingness to write about suffering, the fear to hint even at sadness, as if all our life should be lived under caramel skies." There may be more of that reaction in Russia than we have realized, for the Kremlin recently ordered communist party propagandists to increase their efforts to indoctrinate the people and to combat flirtations with "alien and bourgeois" ideas that would undermine communist power at home.

During 1951 when Presidential nominees were having difficulty getting confirmed by the Senate, James Reston of the New York Times wryly suggested that the nominees observe a few simple rules. Among them were:

"Master various clichés that are popular on Capitol Hill, including the following:

I am for adequate defense, but we must not spend ourselves into bankruptcy.

Glorify the days when we had no entangling alliances. This proves you are a 'sound fellow, longing for the happy sunlit past.'

Stay out of the Far East. If you go there, you will be expected to have views on it and somebody is bound to disagree with any views you have. Ignorance about it, however, is no disqualification."

There was a solid core of truth in this satirical comment. It accurately reflected the American mood of the 1940's and 1950's. There have been reactions against it. Some youngsters have grown beards, worn tight trousers, and read poetry to express their rebellion. Others have put their protests into satire. The beatniks dissent in despair rather than in hope of the future. The beatniks are so opposed to conformity that they think the only way man can call his soul his own is to become an outcast. Still others have sought spiritual affirmation in the religious reawakening we have witnessed.

The storm over the requirement of loyalty oaths and affidavits from college students seeking federal loans is another sign of reawakening. The recent addition of Yale and Harvard to Princeton and the other colleges which had earlier opposed the requirement is a blow for freedom and a powerful protest against the demands of orthodoxy.

There have been other signs of re-examination—increasing discontent with complacency and a feeling of anxiety that impending disaster may be ahead and that the problems of the world are slipping beyond our control. The portrait of America as a nation addicted to country club standards, evasive of controversial issues, dedicated to material ends, and lacking the sense of a great mission has come home to more and more people. As Jane Addams once said: "The most praiseworthy journey grows dull and leaden, unless companioned by youth's iridescent dreams." It is not too late to recapture those dreams.

The Nature of the Competition

We need to do so quickly, for the competition is severe. And the stakes are our civilization itself. The competition is usually thought of in terms of capitalism versus communism. Actually, no pure form of either exists. Even the communism of Soviet Russia has been modified in the interests of food production, by entrusting an important segment of farming to private hands. In Russia there has been an increasing recognition of private property. Two-story family dwellings can be privately owned, and considerable private property passes by will or intestate succession. Our system of public controls, such as farm subsidies, strict regulation of the volume of oil produced, and the provisions for old age, unemployment, and sickness insurance, have greatly modified the classical institution of capitalism. The truth is that the capitalist nations have evolved into a form of collectivism. The basic issues between the competing systems of the world concern freedom of the individual.

I doubt whether either system, the communist or our own, has ceased to evolve. The ultimate issue will be which form of collective society will allow greater scope for individual freedom and the exercise of the individual's mind and talents. Unless we bestir ourselves to understand the many and subtle influences making for conformity within our own system, we cannot be as certain of tomorrow's answer as we think.

We think of initiative as the virtue of the West, a trait nurtured by the contest for money, by the high monetary rewards for those who finish first. There is much truth there, though it is less solid than we imagine. There is severe competition for top awards in the Soviet Union also. Its colleges have room for not more than one-fifth of the high school graduates. Competition to get in is therefore very intense; and competition among the select few to get to the professional top is also very great. Moreover, there is a feeling among millions of Asians that when we give our greatest rewards to those with the best acquisitive instinct we do not necessarily advance the good life. The freedom we cherish and defend embraces, of course, the right to seek opportunities for material things. But it includes also the right to speak, to write, to think, to worship as one pleases, without intervention from the state. It includes the right to be different from the crowd, to walk alone and unafraid, the right at times even to shake a fist at authority. The right to defy an unconstitutional law is, indeed, very deep in our moral and legal tradition.

Freedom in this broad sense is the ultimate aim of the good society. We have the institutions as well as the traditions that make that freedom possible. That is the one overwhelming advantage we have over the communist camps.

Today we do not exploit that advantage. Is freedom no longer a real passion in our lives? How can we be intolerant of minority views and minority groups at home and be partners with unorthodox people in Asia and Africa? How can we cultivate normalcy and mediocrity at home and be revolutionaries abroad?

Toynbee reminds us that great civilizations usually commit suicide. His analysis of the passing of the great Greek civilization in *Civilization on Trial* points to the internal decay that set in when man was deified and human power worshipped. The deadening of individuality, the growth of intolerance, the exaltation of mediocrity, the implicit insistence that our elite think and act like some prototype of Americanism, the insensitivity to the staggering injustices which we have allowed minorities and nonconformists to suffer—these are warnings that our civilization is imperilled. Holmes, with keen insight of the drift, wrote as long ago as 1919, "The whole collectivist tendency seems to be toward underrating or forgetting the safeguards in bills of right that had to be fought for in their day and that still are worth fighting for. . . . We have been comfortable so long that we are apt to take for granted that everything will be all right without our taking any trouble."[7]

We were born in revolution. The right to be different, the revulsion against interference with conscience and beliefs, respect for minorities—these were part of our great moral tradition. We exalted the dissenter or innovator and saved a noble place for him. He challenged the *status quo* and was the agency of change. He is more sorely needed today than ever, because the rate of change is increasing. In simpler days a man's education might carry him through life. Changes are now so rapid that an engineer may be obsolete after ten years and need a new education. It is true in many

[7] Vol. 2, Holmes-Pollock Letters, p. 25.

fields that the worst enemies of progress are the narrow prejudiced views obtained in an education that is now outmoded. The need for constant re-education is greater than ever. Unless we are geared to perform that service, we cannot keep abreast of problems. The challenges of this age exceed any in our history. Yet it seems that we are more and more frozen in attitudes and positions.

We seem immobilized at a time when our inventive genius should be the most active.

A vast proliferation of ideas and radical changes in attitudes are necessary if we are to meet the mounting crises at home and abroad.

We need in truth a genuine revolt against the regimes that have fed us tranquilizers and made us think that all is well abroad and that domestic needs can wait. Revolt is necessary if we are to avoid becoming a second-rate nation.

THE NATION AND THE
WORLD

THERE may have been a time when America by a show of great strength could bend many critical world situations to its will. If that power existed, it was of short duration. Certainly it does not exist today. Yet we often act as if it did—as if we could by some dramatic act or by quick use of our striking power solve the situation in Hungary, manage the problem in China, or quiet the jibes against us in South America. Indeed we often act as if the object of our foreign policy is to bring Mr. Khrushchev to his knees, apologizing in abject terms for his attitude toward Berlin and all the other troubled areas.

The World's Political Center

We deal however with situations largely beyond our power completely to shape according to our own wishes. New powers in the family of nations have emerged or are emerging. The political center of the world is no longer in America. It was Spengler's theory that the political center would leave the West and move East, centering in Moscow, Peking, or Delhi. That has not happened as yet. Neither Moscow nor Peking has achieved that importance today. The political center probably lies in the Atlantic Community. To keep it there will not be easy, since the bulk of the peoples as well as many of the riches of the world are in Asia. Yet until the Asian peoples progress in development and master their vast resources, East and West will offset each other. It is, I think, a situation of equilibrium with which we deal—delicate, changeable, fluctuating. If I am right we are in a better position to negotiate than to dictate.

Problems of Geography

Another sobering fact comes from an observation of the British geographer Mackinder that America is an island far removed from "the heartland" of the earth. The part of the earth having the largest potential for exertion of pressures is Asia. The center of Asia (whose present dynamo is Moscow) marks the point from which in theory the greatest force can be exerted. Easy land approaches link it to Europe, to China, and to the Middle East. Asia is hooked to Africa by land, and it commands off its shores great archipelagoes. There are no oceans to cross to reach any point in this Asian-African land mass. Moscow, dominating this "heartland," has an enormous geographical advantage.

The very presence of powerful Russia to the north of Turkey, Syria, Iraq, Iran, and Afghanistan creates pressures that are incalculable. A few months ago the Russian Ambassador in Teheran threatened Iran with a shower of missiles if she did not bend to Soviet will. More subtle influences are always present, though unseen and unspoken. A small nation bordering mighty Russia will not necessarily knuckle under. But the presence of Russian power so close at hand qualifies and conditions the neighbor's actions and policy. This is leverage that cannot easily be counter-balanced with forces at the command of a nation so distant as ours.

These Middle Easterners like the Russians as people and fear the Soviet Union as a nation. She has never been the model nation. Beginning a century and a half ago she started her southern march, absorbing other nations and biting off huge chunks of Iran. That was Czarist Russia. But manifest destiny in both Czarist Russian and Soviet Russian eyes has been the south with its warm waters and Africa.

South of Russia's Borders

South of the border the feelings about Russia are mixed. There is fear, yet there is also admiration. Travel that border and you will hear that people in Russia can write and read, that they have hospitals for sick people, that all medicines are free, that the cities are modern, that peasants' sons go to college. It's all true. Soviet Russia has gone to great pains to make Central Asia a show place. Baku, Tashkent, and Alma Ata are lovely modern cities. The universities are packed. Illiteracy is practically wiped out. Farms are mechanized. Opera houses are magnificent. These facts, mundane to us, are bright sparkling bits of information for the Middle Eastern peasant who lives in a mud hut, whose wife gives birth in the fields, who has no medical care, who dreams above all else that his offspring may be educated. The incessant rumor in the villages of the Middle East that farmers' sons in Russia become leading doctors and engineers is the most powerful of all propaganda.

The dynamic Soviet economy just across the border has a magnetism hard to overemphasize in this and in other respects. For those of us who have known freedom, a step toward communism would be a step down. That is not necessarily the case with the serfs of the Middle East and Asia. They have never known liberty or justice. They have known only privation, and the bounteous production of the Soviet system seems to them a tremendous advance. Sides will often be chosen in this contest for the hearts and minds of men, not on logic or reason but on a history which has shown that nothing could be worse than what has been endured.

Russian Evangelists

The communist nations have long been preparing citizens of the various countries of the world for communist work abroad. Prague is today an important center for this graduate work. But all communist lands have their universities filled with overseas students. These include Peking as well as Moscow. The courses include commando and jungle warfare, intelligence and subversion, as well as the history of communism and dialectical materialism. Africa today is receiving special attention. Hundreds of Africans are in these schools being prepared for communist work back home.

The Russians sent abroad on various missions are also evangelists. Soviet Russia is equipped and prepared to evangelize like no other nation. She has mastered the languages of the world, and is now fluent in at least sixty-eight of them. The hundreds of African languages and dialects are also coming to be her specialty. Few Russian representatives, either in her foreign service or on her technical staffs, go to a country unless they can speak the local language. We are improving, but in Asia we are lucky if we have ten out of a hundred who can do that. And, as I said, there are several dozen of these languages we are not yet qualified even to teach.

Russia has experts by the tens of thousands prepared for this out-of-country work. She has so many agricultural graduates, engineers, and doctors, she does not know what to do with them. In Moscow these experts are called the "gold reserve." They are invaluable in Russia's programs of internal development; they are the evangelists of the Soviet way of life in other countries. We have a great misconception of them. We think of them as subversive characters, boring from within. Russia has a vast network for espionage, but these experts who work abroad are not of that character. They are professional people who live discreet lives in the communities where they work. Attached to them are commissars to make sure they do not go astray. The Russian technical experts mind their own business and operate at the professional level, building bridges, roads, steel plants, silos and factories that are as good as any we can produce. The subversives, boring from within, are not the Russians but the nationals of the other country who went to Moscow for training and returned home to form the cells of the local communist party.

These Russian experts who go abroad are given preferential salaries. But they need not be coaxed to go. They can be ordered abroad. And unlike many we send, they do not live in air-conditioned houses; they live at the same level as anyone else and gain prestige doing so. These technical emissaries evangelize for Russia by modernizing ancient lands. They install machinery whose spare parts will in the future come from Russia. They help weave the skein that pulls every outlying area closer and closer to Moscow. At present we are neither prepared nor equipped to match this Russian effort. The Atlantic Community, let alone the United States, has not yet seen or understood the true dimensions of this problem.

Communist Enchantment

A more ominous advantage that the Russians enjoy—
and in the sweep of history the Chinese communists
will also share it—is that the underdeveloped nations
are in a curious way more susceptible to communist
enchantment than to democratic persuasion. The reason has nothing to do with the merits of the two systems but to the background of the people. The underdeveloped nations, those that make up the so-called un-
committed people of the world, have always been
bossed, pushed around, controlled by some group.
Perhaps it was a colonial power whose officials ran the
country. It may have been a king or even a church.
The landlord group usually exercised vast authority.
In the Middle East to this day most farmers do not
plow, do not cultivate, do not reap and thrash until
the landlord's representative tells them to do so. They
are accustomed to *authority*; they bow to it. People in
that tradition, folks who have that pattern of thought
and action would not be noticeably disturbed if the
voice that commanded them was the voice of a com-
missar, especially if he was of their race and nationality
(as he assuredly would be) and if his words dripped
with the honey of brotherhood and freedom (as it
probably would at the onset).

People who have long been subject to the voice
of authority might well be lost and dazed when free-

dom suddenly was granted them. Harry Golden in
Only in America tells how the Jews of Europe were
in ghettos for centuries, hammering at the doors
to get out. Yet when they were released, he says,
"there was very great anguish. . . . The security of
the closely knit society was no more. It took hard
work to make your way on your own." In Asia, the
Middle East, and Africa people have long been held
together by numerous ties. Sometimes it was a tribe.
A paternal regime often held sharecroppers securely
under one landlord, the tenants assuming the debts that
their ancestors owed the ancestors of the landlord. In
India it was the caste, which we of the West deride. Yet
these institutions were cementing influences that gave
people a sense of security, a sense of belonging. Once the
old societies are broken up, forces of disintegration go
to work. These people are bewildered and lost, sometimes to such an extent that physical illness results.
They have no anchors, no confidence, no sense of direction, except and unless one of their own people emerges
as a great leader who is imbued with democratic ideals.
Nehru did that in India; and democracy has had a
bright start there, even in the lower echelons of the
villages. But Jinnah in Pakistan died and no magnetic
figure emerged who was both a leader and a man
steeped in democratic traditions. Indonesia, Laos, and
other countries have had experiences like those of Pakistan. And it is certain that some of the newly emerging

countries of Africa will suffer the same pains. Where a people are largely illiterate, where they have long been conditioned to *authority*—indeed dependent on it—he who comes with a democratic program has more obstacles than the communist who parades as "liberator" but substitutes a new yoke of authority for the old one.

Though democracy is not exportable like food and cement, the slogan "one man, one vote" is a contagious one in the newly emerging countries. Literacy and intelligence are not synonymous, for in the general elections of India the people have shown great discernment. Yet across the hills in Pakistan the electorate was greatly corrupted, the illiteracy of the masses being exploited for the benefit of a cabal of selfish men. Pakistanis are not more backward than Indians. The difference is largely in the existence of Nehru who was dedicated and inspired and led his people. Pakistan is now developing a limited form of democracy. The election districts are made up of about 8,000 people who elect officials to manage that unit of government. Those officials in turn select representatives to govern the larger units of government.

In Indonesia there is not even that degree of democracy. A council governs, determining what is best for the people. Some dictatorships born in revolution are taking bizarre forms as in Iraq and Cuba. The illiteracy of people in newly emerging countries, their attitude towards government, their incapacity to understand how capital is formed for industrial development, and their intolerance for minorities place them many decades behind the viable democratic societies in the western world.

We may expect long years of turbulence as these nations acquire the strength to walk on their own legs. A disciplined group is apt to guide and control them— to develop educational programs and to provide capital formation as rapidly as possible. That will be true, I think, in nations where illiteracy is over 50 per cent and where per capita income is as low as $60, $100, $200, $250 a year. The contest in the years ahead will be for control of the elite group which governs these emerging nations. The communists will be ever-present.

Can we develop once more the capacity to think and scheme and collaborate with revolutionaries? Can we develop imaginative ways to woo loud and raucous leaders into democratic programs? Can we learn patience to deal with the crude beginnings of revolutions and through teachers and doctors and nurses help people at village levels lay the foundations for a democratic society? Pouring in money will be as futile as sending marines. The masses coming into the new voting booths are no farther along than the serfs under King John. They need help and tutelage so that they can find within themselves the power to develop democratic institutions that fit their particular needs.

The War of the Ruble

Russia has another advantage over us in this political contest. Because of her system of state-owned enterprise, she can undermine world market prices—sell cheap—by a simple state decision. Free private enterprise that must make its costs can compete only if it has subsidies; which are rarely available. Nations like Afghanistan, that do their financing of industrial projects by issuing more currency, over the long pull actually prefer Russian contracts to American contracts because they cost less. Our private enterprise costs reflect our high standard of living. But the great advantages of this high standard of living put us at times at a competitive disadvantage abroad.

The situation we find ourselves in at this mid-point of the twentieth century is not a bright one. Yet it is not hopeless. The Chinese word for "crisis" is made out of two characters; one is "danger" 危 the other is "opportunity" 機 The present world crisis offers great opportunities to the free world. We need, however, drastically to revise our thinking and our strategy lest the center of political gravity move so far east and the strength of the communist bloc become so great that we are left in a minor insular position with the tides of history sweeping by us.

Money and Guns Not Enough

Plainly the bombs—the ones we now have, the ones we may invent—will not restore the balance to us, for the communist world is at least as strong in that regard and perhaps even stronger. Plainly money cannot buy our way out of the *impasse*. A Marshall Plan saved Europe from disintegration in a dark hour. But Europe was composed of viable democratic societies, of nations with institutions that were fairly representative of the people, with foundations for an excellent industrial plant. Asia and Africa present vastly more complicated problems. The question there is not whether democracy will be saved; it is whether democracy will ever be born. The question is not whether an industrial plant can be repaired; it is whether an industrial society can ever be built. Money, discreetly spent, will be indispensable, but pouring money in can result in the same fiasco as that in China. We could send engineers out and build plants and factories according to American blueprints. But there is no indigenous managerial group, no trained technical staff to operate them. And in many lands there are no democratic institutions, no democratic traditions to give assurance that the plant once built will serve the democratic cause. After all, there is nothing ideological about a cement plant or a steel mill. Communists can build them and use them for their purposes as well as we can for ours. Guns and dollars alone will not do the job. We need imagination and ingenuity to devise new programs of action to meet the threat of communism both at the political and the military level.

Cold War

When I hear some friends talk, I begin to think they have a vested interest in the cold war. When tensions increase, a curious sense of security develops. Hate and suspicion of a foreign influence readily unite people, and united they feel new strength. They are willing to leave knotty problems to the experts in the Pentagon. If we give the military enough money and build bomb shelters at home, perhaps the problems that beset the world will be solved. This is the most dangerous mood a nation today can have. It leads to a slow but steady drift toward the holocaust, for the basic problems of survival at this stage are primarily political. When we forsake or disdain or fail to employ the political ingenuity with which we are blessed, we strengthen the forces that lead to destruction.

Abolition of Nuclear Bombs

We now face the dreadful realities of nuclear bombs that can destroy the life of the planet and render the earth sterile for eons of time. There is the ever-present danger that someone, mad with ambition or fear, will trigger that holocaust. We cannot truly claim moral authority if we fail to exert our utmost in relieving the world of the tensions which that prospect creates. We must lead the international community in the outlawry of nuclear power for military purposes. Once, we alone had the bomb. Now the communist world has broken the monopoly. If the prospects of Soviet use of the bomb seem terrifying, what of the day when Red China fills the skies with planes carrying that kind of warhead? That day is probably much closer than we have imagined. Some think that test explosions are safe if conducted in faraway places—islands too remote to be important in the white man's world, deserts like the Sahara that seem to most people only wastelands where no life grows. But the waters of the South Seas are fishing grounds for many races, and the Japanese fishermen know to their sorrow that fish are now often radioactive. The Moroccan, Mr. Benhima, had a powerful answer to the French when they said they would test their nuclear bombs in the Sahara. The Sahara is a region teeming with life. Several hundred thousands of people who live there are utterly dependent on the oases. If these are made radioactive, the civilization of these people will end. But DeGaulle did not listen. With a loud hurrah the French have exploded their first nuclear bomb in the Sahara, and strong reactions are heard from Ghana, from Morocco, from all over Africa.

We cannot as a people sanction the use of any instrument either for experimentation or for war which makes the soft trade winds, the great refreshing gales

[44]

out of the west, and the gentle rains the agents of death. We cannot stand mute while the air is polluted by explosions, endangering people on all the continents. We must induce all nations to end the testing or use of a missile that destroys not only armies but people whose only sin is breathing the air, eating food from garden plots and farms, and taking fish from the oceans. The bomb kills in agonizing ways. It affects even the genes and produces sick children and monstrosities years hence. We cannot sponsor that instrument of destruction and retain moral authority in the councils of nations. We, rather than the communists, should seize the political initiative and make this our cause, designing the necessary international controls that will make the outlawry as fool-proof as possible.

Yet this step is not enough. The techniques for making these awful engines of destruction have been mastered and are spreading to all lands. If all the existing bombs are collected and destroyed, the risk of nuclear war would still exist. For once any war starts, the temptation will be great for one contestant to end it by using the most powerful instrument of destruction the world has known.

The experts seem to agree that even if all nuclear warheads were destroyed there would be nuclear warfare if war broke out. For those weapons are so decisive, the side that has them will win. Now that the know-how for making them exists, they can be made in thirty to ninety days. The testimony on the effects indicates that 1,500 megatons would kill 30% of our population. But we would not be the ones to choose the amount which would be loosened on us. A 20,000 megaton attack on the United States would kill 95% of us and, if casualties are excluded, only 3% of us would survive. There are those who try to build up our hopes by pointing out that perhaps only 50% of us would be killed and only our cities destroyed—if we now planned caves in rural areas for the other 50%. This is the rosiest side of the picture that can be drawn. Yet it must be remembered that nuclear bombs are merely one of a senior group of weapons. Bacteriological and chemical weapons are also emerging.

Prevention of War

The only sure way to prevent the use of nuclear weapons is to prevent war. If a war starts, we cannot be certain what weapons will be used before it ends, irrespective of paper agreements or solemn pledges. We need progressive disarmament cutting back all arms in a balanced way. We need especially to have balanced disarmament in the sensitive and dangerous areas of the world. We need to have something short of massive retaliation to use in local situations where an aggressor will be apt to halt once his bluff is called.

The Rule of Law

The prevention of war requires the invention of political devices and institutions which are substitutes for a clash of arms. We have gone far in exploiting our scientific genius. But our political genius has not kept pace with our scientific achievements. There has been nothing as radical or new in the field of government as our startling achievements in nuclear physics. One rough measure of our deficiency in providing international controls of common problems is evidenced by the fact that last year the International Court at The Hague had only six cases to adjudicate, the highest number before it in a decade. Its rulings often are advisory only, as most nations give qualified acceptances to its jurisdiction.[8]

We must forsake that insular attitude. We must start in earnest to exploit our political inventiveness if the holocaust is to be avoided.

We cannot expect a world system of law suddenly to appear full-blown and adequate for all contingencies. We must, however, make advances that are as revolutionary as the hydrogen bomb, if we are to develop rules of law under which nations can live in peace. We on this continent adopted a federation composed of sovereign nations, and we provided the Supreme Court

[8] See *International Court of Justice, Yearbook 1958-1959*, pp. 205 et seq; Lissitzyn, The International Court of Justice (1951) pp. 61-68.

as the tribunal for settlement of controversies between them. We can inaugurate the beginnings of a like rule of law in the international field by a few simple expedients. President Eisenhower's proposal to submit all disputes under treaties to the International Court with power on its part to render binding decisions is one place to commence. That device can be evolved to include many types of controversies, including territorial problems that now raise the specter of nuclear war. International institutions can be created to control and administer certain common problems. Nuclear energy is one. We must start now to provide specific procedural devices to adjudicate international controversies and to control and administer such crucial problems as the use of nuclear energy, which all nations have in common. We must in other words carry a "rule of law" beyond the conversation stage and begin to reduce it to specific, concrete forms, if war is to be prevented.

Coexistence

No one but a dreamer would think the ambitions of communist nations would abate even by disarmament. While we need protection against the holocaust and while we need military power to fight if necessary, we also need time in which to develop our political strength and to launch new vitalizing political projects in cooperation with India, with Israel, with Turkey, with Ghana, and with all other democratic societies within and without the Atlantic Community. Indeed we must enlarge our active allies to include the entire Democratic World Community.

Much has been written about "coexistence" as if it would presage a tranquil era devoid of clashes. I do not share that view. The differences between the two systems that now compete are so deep and vast that all of them cannot be eradicated. Negotiation can restrict the areas of conflict and provide temporary arrangements or expedients by which each side can live without apparent surrender of principle, while we hope that time will solve the insolubles. Negotiation with Stalin would probably have been fruitless. Negotiation with Khrushchev probably has more promise. There is hope that negotiation—and the emergence of a "rule of law"—can produce peace in the sense that peace means the absence of world war. There is this, however, to remember. Khrushchev is no less a communist than Lenin and perhaps a better one than Stalin. For Khrushchev is an evangelist at the world level and a master propagandist. He does more than preach; he presents the Soviet Union as a model of achievement for the underdeveloped nations, a benefactor of the needy through foreign aid and trade, an eager victor over the United States in the race of technology and production. Khrushchev has some prestige on his side, for at this level sputnik argues for him.

Yet there is, I feel, an important role that negotiation

can perform. It can inaugurate the beginnings of a "rule of law." Negotiation can eliminate some sore spots and reduce others. Negotiation can result in larger and more stimulating interchanges between peoples as well as between governments. Negotiation can build many bridges of understanding between the two competing groups. Negotiation may even produce cooperative undertakings which will make the International Geophysical Year seem quite minor.

One product of cooperation between the West and the Soviets may be that Russia can be made to become an effective policeman for all Asia. Russia has need for peace in that sector. She has positions of prestige to maintain in the Asian community. Red China is a Russian problem too. It may indeed loom larger in Russian minds as the years unfold than it does in Indian or Japanese minds. Americans do not know much of Russian history. But Khrushchev does. He knows that the Mongols under the house of Batu held suzerainty over Moscow for two hundred years beginning in 1236 A.D. Russia and China with a common border of great length may live as peacefully during the next century as Canada and the United States; but the explosive forces at work in China, including a rapid rise in population, will in the long run create dangerous problems on Russia's eastern border. Why, otherwise, is Russia settling her recently discharged soldiers on her eastern borders? If we dream of designing a diplomacy that will pit Russia against China in a war that will destroy each, we are doomed to failure. Indeed, such a policy would be likely to intensify feelings against us in both Russia and China. If we plan to get on such terms with Russia as to encourage her as a peacemaker in Asia, there is more prospect of fulfillment. Nations usually act out of self-interest, not idealism. There are many areas in which Russia's self-interest will be found identical to ours. Those we should exploit.

But the clash of ideologies will continue for years. Time alone will strike a true balance. Time alone will erode the passion for making all faiths bow to the communist will. The situation is not unique in history. Islam on one side and Christian Europe on the other were long at swords' points. In that contest submission or extinction was the goal. Time cured that situation. Time will cure the present one, at first making conditions more malleable and at long last making them wholly negotiable. We are now only at the beginning of the transition and nowhere near the end.

We need a passion for peace and a willingness to conciliate all possible differences. We need such a passion for peace that we forego truculence, take the lead in formulating a "rule of law" for international disputes, and cultivate desires to conciliate international differences. It also means, until *bona fide* disarmament

133000

on a gradual scale can be worked out, the maintenance of a position of military strength.

Our political program needs at least the same top priority as the military one, in terms of our planning and budgeting. There is no precise program or blueprint we can hope to follow. We will need to improvise, to alter, to take new tactics. The secret of success will be to keep alive at home a ferment of ideas that will produce innovations abroad. We will need constant reappraisal of any project we launch. We must be flexible and resourceful. Each program we fashion must be geared to domestic and world realities.

Economic Growth

The problem of economic growth is a leading political one. In the world of today this is no longer purely an internal matter of deciding how rapidly we can increase our affluence. It is primarily an international problem, basically influencing and influenced by our defense and foreign policy. Yet, despite this importance, our Government has no growth policy worth the name, trusting that if only the budget is balanced at the lowest possible level, the "hidden hand" will produce the rate of growth that is best fitted to our internal and international requirements. No decision has been made whether a growth rate of $3\frac{1}{2}\%$ per year, corresponding to our experience during the last decade, and also during the past 120 years, is enough. Must we not do better in a world where the Soviet Union has been expanding its national income during the last decade twice as fast as we have? There is little doubt that with sufficient determination and the right policies we could increase our average rate of growth to 4% per year, and possibly even close to 5%, within a basically free enterprise economy. This would still be well below the Soviet rate of growth which is expected to lie between 6% and 7%; but the difference at least would not be as sharp as it is likely to be if we continue the policy of drift and apathy. From the global point of view the allocation of the increase in national product is as important as the overall rate of growth. What makes Soviet economic growth a challenge to us is not only, or even primarily, the size of its aggregate output ten or twenty years hence, when it will still be below ours, but the fact that the Soviet Union can and does allocate a considerably larger share of total national product to the sectors that matter in today's power struggle: (1) to modern armaments and (2) to those that increase future product, such as investment and education.

The Soviets leave roughly a bit more than one-third of their gross national product for consumption.

We are a smaller nation in terms of total population and our gross national product is about three times that of the Soviets. We divide our gross national product approximately as follows: two thirds for consumption; one sixth for investment; one sixth for defense and government. We apparently work on the assumption that the more we eat, the more gadgets we can buy, etc., the better we can fight communism in the world. But these antics of ours are wholly irrelevant to the contest for men's minds and hearts in the outer reaches of the earth. How much we eat will have no effect on the global contest. What will count are: (1) how much we can put into our own growth so that we will forge constantly ahead; and (2) how much we can have ready to promote democratic movements in India, Ghana, Bolivia, and elsewhere.

These are matters of primary concern lest the United States become a second-rate power. We must do two things: (1) keep strong militarily and be able to carry our share of aid to underdeveloped nations; (2) expand greatly in our services to our own people. It is startling to realize we have a burgeoning population and yet no adequate school facilities at the primary, secondary, college, post-graduate, or research levels. We have automobiles but not the highway structures to accommodate them. Our wilderness areas are inadequate; our rivers are dreadfully polluted. We have mounting needs for hospitals and medical care, yet our facilities to fill these needs are greatly deficient. The amounts we spend on research on cancer, blood and liver disorders, tuberculosis, and other diseases, are mere pittances to what we should be spending. What we are doing in housing is far below the national needs, especially at the slum level. Walter Lippmann put it all in a nutshell recently when he said that our controlling principle at least for the last seven years has been to put "private comfort and private consumption ahead of national need" and to reduce "the share of the national income devoted to public purposes." And he added, "The challenge of the Soviet Union has been demanding an increase, not a reduction, of the share of the national income devoted to public purposes. We are falling behind because we are not allowed to run."

That is why the national power of the Soviets is forging ahead of our national power. The Soviet economy, though only half as big as ours, is growing twice as fast.

Unless we boost our growth rate, we will do no more than hold our own. Holding our own is not enough. Formulation of a national growth policy and designing incentives to accelerate it are among our foremost needs.

Problems of Underdeveloped Nations

Only 15% of the people of the world earn more than $450 a year. The vast majority live out their lives below what we of the West think of as the subsistence level. Fifteen cents a day per person is India's average, and she is not alone in that low bracket. Fifteen cents a day is shorthand for deficiencies in food, medicines, hospitals, schools, playgrounds, parks, factories, roads, housing and so on. These underdeveloped lands are primarily agricultural. Eighty per cent or more live on the land. The less than 8% that produces America's food is vastly more efficient. These nations must in the long run transform their agricultural societies to industrial-agricultural societies, if they are to raise their living standards. That will take years on end, since we start with nations who often do not even have plumbers, not to mention automobile mechanics or skilled workers who can repair farm machinery. Selling them farm machinery will come in time. But it is usually the worst first step since they are not equipped to use it.

Food

The first requirement is food. Much can be done abroad on this food problem by private agencies. In 1943 the Rockefeller Foundation began a program in cooperation with the Mexican government to increase the production of that country's staple food commodities. From the beginning the key principles have been education and cooperation. Direct aid in the form of food, plants, or equipment has played no part.

Agricultural specialists sent by the Foundation from the United States conduct research and experimentation in the development of new strains of corn, wheat, and other staples and the development of modern techniques of fertilization, pest and disease control, and farm management which are specially adapted to the Mexican land, climate, and economy. Recent graduates of the local agricultural colleges participate in every phase of the program. Many of these young men and women are sent, after a period of training, to a United States university for additional study and research on fellowships provided by the Foundation. These young people, steeped in agricultural science and research techniques, are then taken into private industry or government agencies where they can spread their knowledge and put it to practical use.

The research operations revolve about an experimental farm of a few hundred acres, complete with greenhouses and field laboratories. All operations are coordinated with studies at the agricultural colleges; and the Mexican extension service, similar to our own county agent system, is provided with the results to be passed on to the farmers. Results of the research are also widely publicized in trade journals, and people from other Latin American countries are brought to Mexico to observe the experiments in progress.

Few, if any, Latin American countries have not profited from the Mexican operation. Yet the tangible results in Mexico alone are phenomenal. In only seventeen years, food production in Mexico has nearly doubled. Wheat production, for example, has tripled. Whereas Mexico imported half a million tons of wheat in 1944, far more than it produced, present production is at the rate of a million and a half tons and importation is no longer necessary. The rate of growth in food production comfortably exceeds the rate of population increase and the improved diet of the Mexican people has already shown up in the vital statistics.

Although the Foundation has also carried on extensive operations in Colombia and Chile, the total cost of its entire Latin American program has been less than fifteen million dollars—the price of a few jet planes—a sum which would have furnished outright only about 300,000 tons of wheat, a fifth of last year's Mexican output.

The efficient use of money is not the only advantage to this approach to foreign aid. It is, indeed, a minor one. This kind of operation does no damage to national pride; in fact, it nourishes national pride. Moreover, the benefits are lasting. Soon it is expected that Mexico's own experts, trained by the Foundation, will be able to take over the operation and assume full responsibility for the continuous improvement of the country's agriculture. What has been done in Mexico can be done in country after country.

Survival is the urgent political need of any people. The farm surpluses of America constitute our most important political asset in these early years. Often, however, the food we raise is not the kind people in Asia or Africa need. We must restudy our farm problem with this in mind. We must gear our farm production to world needs, raising what the deficit nations such as India desire to eat.

This food problem is not a short range one. It will

be important in the years ahead. Asia's population is burgeoning. Red China adds fifteen million people a year to her population; India adds six million. India may need for the indefinite future at least five million tons of wheat and rice a year. She will need it in advance of actual market demands so she can store it. Word of grain shortages in Asia sends prices soaring and makes people panicky. Asia needs new granaries that can be kept full. Full granaries level off market prices and put people at ease.

We must also make an effort to help introduce scientific agriculture to at least the heavily populated areas. Many feel that India is not overpopulated but merely underfertilized. She is basically on a vegetarian diet. An acre of land will feed three or more times the number of people who are vegetarians than those who are meat eaters. India, with twice the population of our own, farms about the same amount of land. If she used the amount of fertilizer we use and Europe uses, she might well have a food surplus at present population levels. Chemical plants to process the fertilizers, experts say, are India's greatest need.

Meanwhile the more fortunate nations will be asked to help feed all nations where hunger is the central problem. We must, indeed, plan with other nations how to use wisely our respective food surpluses. The United States and Canada, as well as most European nations, have some food in surplus. Burma has a rice surplus. There will be others with food for the world market. We must collaborate to plan world food needs together and to market the food surpluses intelligently. No nation can act wisely alone. Joint action in the Democratic World Community is necessary. We cannot let hungry people starve, whatever their race or their politics. Hunger produces the deepest cleavages there are in the world. We never can afford to let loose the hatred that hungry people have for him who shuts the door of the granary in their faces. It is food, I think, that in the long run will build a bridge of good-will between us and the six hundred million Chinese on the mainland.

The population trend, due to medical discoveries and widespread advances in sanitation, is moving upward at an alarming rate. World population is increasing by 5,400 every hour, by 47,000,000 a year. It took the world from the beginning to about 1830 to produce a population of one billion people. It is now close to three billion. At the present rate it will be six billion by the year 2000. Then there will be as many Chinese in the world as there are people today. America's food bank in the long run may not be enough. But in the years immediately ahead we will have surpluses, and we must plan to use them wisely in the political contest that will continue for years on end.

Planes versus Hospitals and Schools

The Pentagon announced last year that it had given Ethiopia twelve jet fighter planes. Jet fighter planes to fight whom? The miserable masses of Ethiopia who are 98% illiterate? What feelings of resentment these people must have against America when these multi-million dollar planes land and take off next to mud huts as miserable as any in the world! It is said that Bolivia (55% illiterate) will get jet fighter planes as gifts from the American people. To fight whom? The people? The amount any illiterate nation will spend training pilots to fly the jet planes is badly needed in its budget for education.

When I read of such gifts they seem so wasteful as to be shameful. Why don't we take a fraction of the amounts invested in jet fighter planes and establish hospitals or schools in these countries? Then at least we would have achieved a minor victory in the cold war.

That is a natural first reaction. It is, however, an oversimplification. Problems are not solved by the mere grant or loan of money. The major problems of most newly emerging countries are not entirely economic. They start with the need to develop viable societies along democratic lines. This includes the maintenance of a system of checks and balances. It means restraints on the powers of majorities and the protection of minorities. It means an independent judiciary.

Some countries are filled with racial and religious hatreds that are so powerful as to endanger any full-fledged democratic development. Minorities experience daily discrimination. The idea of equal justice may have been powerful when the common enemy was a colonial empire that held all the people down. Yet when liberation comes, the majority often dilutes that concept of equal justice and turns the powers of government to its own advantage.

Moreover, young nations have not developed traditions and habits of thought that propel them along democratic lines. Even criticisms of a Prime Minister may loom as a monstrous offense, and freedom of speech and of press are made to suffer. In these and many other ways the rights of man are again put in jeopardy, once independence is acquired. The American example is, therefore, of continuing importance both at home and abroad.

Education

Whether the problem is economic or political, the solution is creating the power within the people of a nation to solve their own poblems. This means education, whether the problem be health, farming, industry, or government. If we start building factories alone, we start at the wrong end. The basic requirement is for teachers and schools.

We are not yet on the same wave length with the

masses who live in the slums of the earth. The peon in Cuba makes $18 a year; the householder in Kerala—India's troublesome state—makes $24 a year; the national average in India, Nigeria, and Ethiopia is $60; Iran, $150; Vietnam, $100; Thailand, $75; Burma, $50. Eighty-five per cent of the world's people have an annual income of less than $450 a year. How are we going to learn to talk with them? How can we get through to them the image of America's bright conscience and warm heart? How can they ever learn that it is our passion for freedom, not our automobiles and thick steaks that makes us distinguished among nations? We cannot go there and speak their language for we are not yet the linguists of the world. Few among us can harangue a street crowd in Urdu, Hindi, Persian, or even Russian. Carl Sandburg's *Abraham Lincoln* is not available in Hindi, Urdu, Telegu, Tamil, Persian, Arabic, or any of 60 other languages needed for reaching the masses. There are a few books we publish in Asian and African languages; but they are mostly beyond the reach of people just learning to read. Our prices run from 10 cents to one dollar a book. These are steep for a household which has an income of only 15 cents a day.

Yet if we cannot bring the image of America home to the masses, how can we compete with the communists who have native agitators in every street crowd?

Our educational program for underdeveloped nations

should therefore have the same priority as the missile program. Asians and Africans must come here by the tens of thousands, or our teachers must go abroad by the thousands, if these new nations are to have the leaders they need. The life of these foreign students in our colleges, or the life of our teachers abroad, will do more to transmit our democratic ideals than the Voice of America could do with untold millions at its command. In those ways we can build the close intellectual nexus which our society must have with the new nations, if democratic ideas are to be vital in those new regimes.

American Evangelists—People to People

We need to induce tens of thousands of our people to spend some of their years abroad on educational and technical missions. This should be an organized campaign reaching into every college. Extensive preparation will be necessary if our emissaries are to be effective. It means mastering all the languages of the world. In Russia a language expert is given five years of training. Some of it concerns, of course, grammar and vocabulary. But the language expert goes deep into the history and culture of the other nation. When he arrives at his foreign post, he not only speaks the language but is anchored in the customs and traditions of the other people. We need the same imaginative project in every language that people speak on earth. We must become the great linguists of the world. The people we send abroad under that program can do more than all our embassies and legations in translating the American ideals of democracy and justice, making them vivid by example.

We need an institute, perhaps several, such as Dr. James Yen is establishing in the Philippines, where men and women of all underdeveloped nations can come and learn the rudiments necessary for revolutionizing the villages in which they live. Democracy at the grass roots is essential. The job does not end in training engineers, doctors, and university professors. Village workers need to know the elements of first aid, the basic principles of public health, the techniques of scientific agriculture adapted to the needs of the particular area, the methods of organizing village people for self-government. Dr. Yen is wise in establishing his institute in the Philippines. It must be close to the people. New York, Berkeley, and Dallas are as far as Mars from the realities of village life in Asia and Africa. The institutes for village workers must be in and a part of the rice fields; they must be geared to the actual village conditions and mirror faithfully village problems—whether they be the community well that is infected by drainage of surface water, the manner in which outhouses are constructed, or the problems of building sanitary fly-proof homes out of bamboo, reeds, mud, or grass. These institutes will be training centers for village workers. Courses may last only a few months or a year. The trainees will return to their countries with some insight into modern agriculture. They will have a few keys to knowledge; they will know some of the mysteries of modern science that villagers have never known; they will have some vision of what democratic organization is and how it can be achieved.

We tend to think of these foreign projects as the affairs for government. Much of what must be done should be undertaken by private groups, not the government. People-to-people is by far the best way of helping underdeveloped nations. That is what the Rockefeller Foundation has proved in Mexico. That is the way Dr. Yen operates in the Philippines. His group (The International Mass Education Movement, Inc., of which I am a member) is privately supported. We work in turn with a private group in the Philippines known as the Philippine Rural Reconstruction Movement. Occasionally the blessing of the foreign government is necessary. But the group of Americans working on those Islands in the Mass Education program has no contract or arrangement with any of our government agencies. That is by far the best arrangement. The more done by people rather than officials, the better. For government action often carries a stigma of foreign intervention in domestic affairs. Once that impression is created in countries sensitive to the practices of colonialism, emotions run wild and the communist opposition makes political capital.

Foreign Aid

American private enterprise has often made its own arrangements with foreign governments to do the necessary construction work. Some ventures of this character have been profitable to both parties. The appearance of American contractors on the foreign scene will continue. We often hear that what the underdeveloped nations need is capital. Yet they need *expertise* or know-how as badly as they need investment. It is know-how that American private enterprise can furnish. The overseas flow of American technical knowledge and information on modern business methods is under way on a large scale and promises to increase. In some areas American private enterprise can and will make investments too. Yet many new countries have elements of instability that make private investors shy away. As Professor Vernon of Harvard has recently said, "With a few interesting exceptions, the large American corporation of today is not attuned to unusual risks for unusual profits."[9]

The financial undertakings necessary for these new industrial plants will therefore often be too great or too risky for private groups. Here government must play the dominant role. But the United States seldom should act alone; and the total burden is far too great for any one nation to bear. The estimates of the need

[9] Mason, *The Corporation in Modern Society*, 1959, p. 248.

vary. It is probably conservative to say that a hundred billion dollars will be needed in the next decade. The United Nations, the World Bank, or some new institution conceived by the free world must do the financing. The officials who go abroad to administer or supervise the projects should be people of many nations. The appearance of a group of American officials, exerting their influence behind the scenes, would thus be avoided. Colonies of foreigners of one nationality, so harmful to public relations, would not develop. The borrower is then a beneficiary of community aid, not beholden to one great power; and the loan does not get implicated with a single nation's foreign policy. The undertaking is so vast and the requirements so great that the task is one for all industrialized nations. The underdeveloped nations should be wards of the entire group of countries that have their plant built. Russia, a rising giant in industry, eventually may be persuaded to become an active partner with the others.

If the modern developments in Mexico, Turkey, Brazil and to some extent India and Pakistan are reliable guides, heavy governmental investment may stimulate private enterprise. What Professor Vernon calls "government-induced growth"[10] may well be the necessary ingredient for developing private enterprise in many underdeveloped regions.

[10] Mason, *The Corporation in Modern Society*, 1959, p. 259.

[68]

Common Market

Perhaps the greatest single boost for the growth of private enterprise in these newly emerging nations will be the development of a common market, as Will Clayton recently said. A vital element in the cement which has held our nation together is the national area of free trade which the Constitution envisaged and which the Supreme Court, starting with Marshall's opinions in *Gibbons v. Ogden*[11] and *Brown v. Maryland*,[12] upheld. Without this area of free trade the States would likely have erected customs and tariff barriers which would have Balkanized us and set region against region.

The Democratic World Community needs a common market for its long term survival. There is a beginning in the Inner Six and the Outer Seven in Europe. Five Central American nations—Guatemala, Nicaragua, Costa Rica, Honduras, and El Salvador—have created a similar common market. Brazil, Argentina, Mexico, Chile, Peru, Bolivia, Paraguay and Uruguay are in the process of negotiating one to be effective over a twelve-year period. No common market can be created overnight. It takes years—a decade or more—to do it, for the adjustments necessary are often difficult and troublesome. Yet in the long view it must be done for all the free world and we must become participants lest the

[11] 9 Wheat. 1. [12] 12 Wheat. 419.

United States stand alone as an island surrounded by a sea of poverty and hunger.

Over twenty new nations have emerged as independent countries since World War II. They need new industries and a world market where they can get food for the products of their factories. It is doubtful if they can survive against the world's tariff walls. The communist countries will rescue them, but rescue by the communists through trade agreements means political subservience or an uneasy status such as Finland has suffered.

A common market enjoyed by the entire Democratic World Community will mean in time a solidarity and a cohesion throughout the free world which nothing else can provide. The newly emerged countries that are in a common market will be able for the first time to attract private investment. They will quickly develop bonds and patterns of cooperative action which will make for a unity that no amount of money and no amount of speeches can create.

America's Advantages in the Political Contest

America must experience an awakening to do these things. We must shake off the mood of complacency. We must once more be unafraid of new ideas. We must encourage argument and debate, stifling no expressions of views or attitudes. We need a genuine national ferment beginning in our schools and extending through